First Facts®

OUR GOVERNMENT

THE STATE GOVERNOR

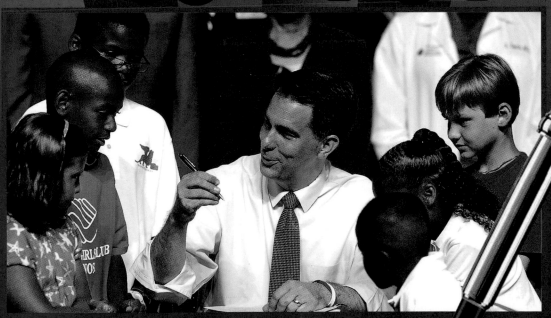

BY JACK MANNING

CAPSTONE PRESS
a capstone imprint

First Facts are published by Capstone Press,
1710 Roe Crest Drive, North Mankato, Minnesota 56003
www.capstonepub.com

Library of Congress Cataloging-in-Publication Data
Cataloging information on file with the Library of Congress
ISBN 978-1-4914-0335-8 (library binding)
ISBN 978-1-4914-0339-6 (paperback)
ISBN 978-1-4914-0343-3 (eBook PDF)

Editorial Credits
Brenda Haugen, editor; Heidi Thompson, designer; Eric Gohl, media researcher;
Katy LaVigne, production specialist

Photo Credits
AP Photo: Alan Diaz, 17, Brian Passino, 1 (left), Sue Ogrocki, cover; Newscom: Danita Delimont
Photography/David R. Frazier, 21, EPA/Roy Dabner, 11, UPI/Bill Greenblatt, 9, 15; Shutterstock:
Aneese, 19, Christopher Halloran, 13, Glam, 7, Jorge Salcedo, cover (background), Krylovochka, 7,
Lev Radin, 5, Vtls, cover (pen), 1 (right)

Printed in China by Nordica
0414/CA21400593
032014   008095NORDF14

TABLE OF CONTENTS

CHAPTER 1

KEEPING PEOPLE SAFE

Does your state have laws that help keep you safe? Keeping **citizens** safe is one of the most important duties for a state governor. State governors often sign new laws to keep kids safe. In Oregon the governor signed a law about wearing safety helmets. Kids in that state must wear safety helmets when using inline skates, skateboards, or scooters.

citizen—a member of a country, state, or city who has the right to live there

CHAPTER 2

STATE GOVERNMENT

State government has three parts. The legislative branch writes **bills** that can become state laws. The judicial branch decides what the laws mean.

The executive branch leads state government. It works with all of the branches. This branch makes sure people follow state laws. The governor is the leader of the state's executive branch.

bill—a written idea for a new law

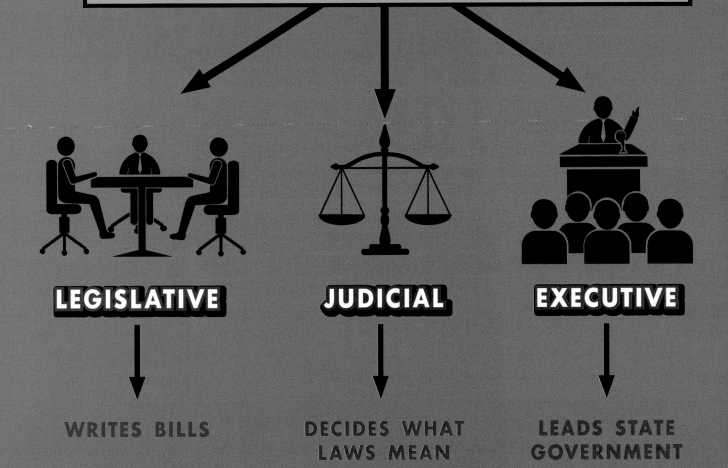

STATE GOVERNMENT

LEGISLATIVE

WRITES BILLS

JUDICIAL

DECIDES WHAT
LAWS MEAN

EXECUTIVE

LEADS STATE
GOVERNMENT

CHAPTER 3

GOVERNORS ARE LEADERS

As leaders of their states, governors have a lot to do. They are in charge of their states' **military**. They sign bills into laws or **veto** them. Governors share ideas on how to spend state money. They choose some state leaders.

military—the armed forces of a state or country
veto—the power or right to stop a bill from becoming law

A governor (right, center) talks with state lawmakers.

CHAPTER 4

WHO CAN BE GOVERNOR

People must follow state rules to become governor. Governors must live in the states they serve. They have to be U.S. citizens. They must be at least 25 years old. In some states governors must be at least 30 years old.

FACT Before taking office many governors served as state lawmakers.

A governor looks over some paperwork.

CHAPTER 5

ELECTING GOVERNORS

Before an **election candidates** share ideas with citizens. They let people know how they will make their state better. On Election Day people **vote** for the candidate they want to be governor.

election—the process of choosing someone or deciding something by voting
candidate—a person who runs for office
vote—to make a choice in an election

The candidate who gets the most votes is elected governor. In many states a governor's **term** lasts four years. In other states a governor's term is two years.

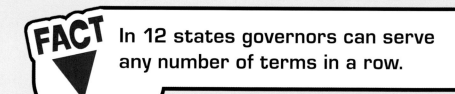

FACT In 12 states governors can serve any number of terms in a row.

term—a set period of time that elected leaders serve in office

A candidate enjoys his win.

BUSY DAYS

Governors have busy days filled with meetings. They meet with state lawmakers to decide how to spend money. They also talk about bills.

Governors meet with people in their states too. They visit schools to talk with teachers and students. Governors listen to everyone's ideas.

WORKING AT THE CAPITOL

Most governors work in offices at their state capitols. Governors study bills in their offices. They make phone calls and read letters. Governors also talk to state lawmakers.

 **FACT** Seventeen governors have gone on to be president of the United States.

HELPING GOVERNORS

Governors choose people to help them. These leaders are in charge of the states' schools, health care, and roads. Lieutenant governors lead most states when governors cannot. They also work on bills with governors and state lawmakers.

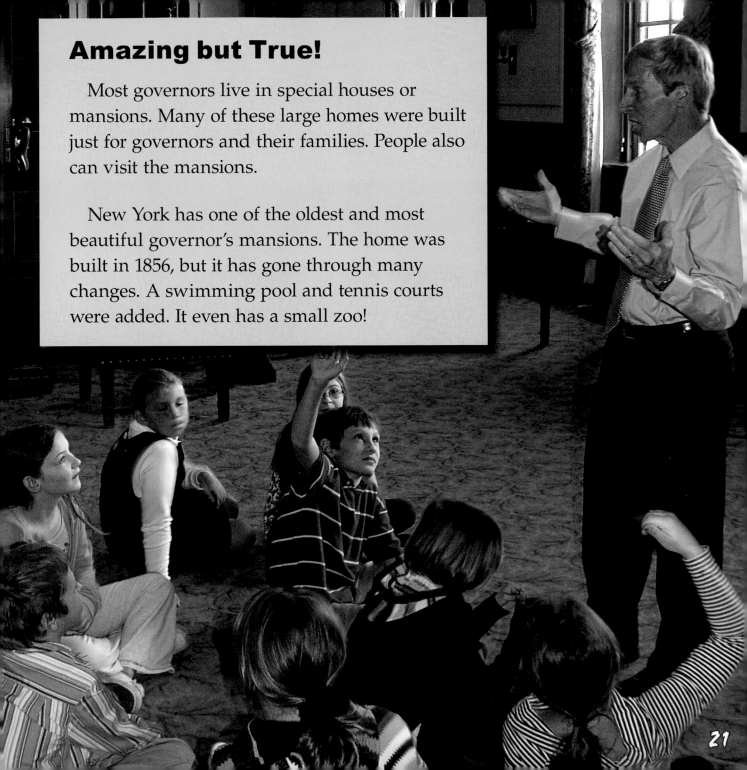

Amazing but True!

Most governors live in special houses or mansions. Many of these large homes were built just for governors and their families. People also can visit the mansions.

New York has one of the oldest and most beautiful governor's mansions. The home was built in 1856, but it has gone through many changes. A swimming pool and tennis courts were added. It even has a small zoo!

GLOSSARY

bill (BIL)—a written idea for a new law

candidate (KAN-di-date)—a person who runs for office

citizen (SIT-i-zuhn)—a member of a country, state, or city who has the right to live there

election (i-LEK-shuhn)—the process of choosing someone or deciding something by voting

military (MIL-uh-tayr-ee)—the armed forces of a state or country

term (TERM)—a set period of time that elected leaders serve in office

veto (VEE-toh)—the power or right to stop a bill from becoming law

vote (VOHT)—to make a choice in an election

READ MORE

Bright-Moore, Susan. *How Is a Government Elected?* Your Guide to Government. New York: Crabtree Pub., 2009.

Gagne, Tammy. *The Power of the States.* My Guide to the Constitution. Hockessin, Del.: Mitchell Lane Publishers, 2012.

Jakubiak, David J. *What Does a Governor Do?* How Our Government Works. New York: PowerKids Press, 2010.

INTERNET SITES

FactHound offers a safe, fun way to find Internet sites related to this book. All of the sites on FactHound have been researched by our staff.

Here's all you do:

Visit *www.facthound.com*

Type in this code: 9781491403358

Check out projects, games and lots more at
www.capstonekids.com

 Super-cool stuff!

INDEX

CRITICAL THINKING USING THE COMMON CORE

1. Governors have busy days filled with meetings. Who do they meet with? Why do they meet with them? (Key Ideas and Details)
2. Governors sign laws to keep people safe. If you were governor, what laws would you sign to keep kids safe? Say why. (Integration of Knowledge and Ideas)